THE BLOOD TYPE
COOKBOOK

*Easy, Healthy and Delicious Recipes
for the Whole Family*

ROBERTA L. KLINE, MD

with JOE R. VELTMANN, PhD

Photographs: © 2014 Roberta L. Kline

On the cover: Macadamia Nut Crusted Baked Cod

Photograph of Dr. Roberta Kline credit Lynn A. Damon

Other titles referenced in this book:

The Moosewood Cookbook © 1977 by Molly Katzen. Ten Speed Press, PO Box 7123, Berkeley CA 94707
ISBN 0-913668-68-0

Eat Right 4 Your Type: The Individualized Diet Solution to Staying Healthy, Living Longer and Achieving Your Ideal Weight © 1996 by Dr. Peter J. D'Adamo with Catherine Whitney. Hoop-a-Joop LLC. G.P. Putnam's Sons, Published by the Penguin Group Inc., 375 Hudson St, New York, NY 10014.
ISBN 0-399-14255-X

This book is lovingly dedicated to my daughters, Marissa and Selena, who have taught me so much and continue to be sources of inspiration and support.

May you always listen to your intuition, follow your heart, and live your dreams.

TABLE OF CONTENTS

Indulgent Endings: Desserts for Your Sweet Tooth

Little Extras

Want More Recipes? Get Connected!

Praise for

THE BLOOD TYPE
COOKBOOK

& Dr. Roberta Kline

When it comes to putting healthy and tasty meals on the table, the most meaningful praise often comes from the people whom you most often entertain—friends, colleagues and family.

"I am grateful to Dr. Kline for being the kind of doctor who treats her patients as individuals with individual health needs. She recognizes that there is no "one size fits all" solution when working with people's health. She considers the whole person, including their genetics and health goals, to provide personalized recommendations including supplements, dietary and lifestyle changes to help improve quality of life for her patients. I'm looking forward to bringing her culinary wisdom into my kitchen with *The Blood Type Cookbook*."

- MELISSA LOTSTEIN

"As a family physician who has been in practice for over 35 years it was my good fortune to meet and be able to work closely with Roberta (Bobbi) Kline, MD. As I practice both conventional and functional medicine, it is a rare gift to come in contact with another holistic physician and healer who exemplifies what I believe to be desperately needed in medicine today. Dr. Kline truly understands the mind-body-spirit connection. She lives this trilogy daily and one of her main beliefs and practices is that diet is one of the cornerstones to creating health. Through her work with our family medicine residency program, she has brought not only her experience and expertise in personalized medicine, genomics and epigenetics to us, she also has reminded us of the need to eat healthy not just at home but at our meetings and events. She is so committed to this end she actually orchestrated a healthy dinner for our students and residents. Her dishes surprised those students who never knew healthy food could taste so delicious. We're all eager to try more of Dr. Bobbi's recipes from *The Blood Type Cookbook*."

- NICHOLAS J. PALERMO, D.O., M.S.
Program Director, Eastern Connecticut Family Medicine Residency Program; Associate Regional Assistant Dean, UNECOM; Functional Medicine Consultant Manchester, CT

"Dr. Kline is brilliant in her ability to listen, assess and integrate all facets of personal health and wellbeing—physical, emotional, nutritional, genetic and spiritual—into meaningful and practical lifestyle guidance. I trust and have been following Dr. Kline's dietary guidance based on blood type for quite some time, feeling better and more energetic each day. It is so exciting to finally have these wonderful recipes at my fingertips in *The Blood Type Cookbook*."

- JUDY IMPERATORE

"Dr. Kline truly offers personalized healthcare in a way that I have never experienced before. Without her I would not be in the healthy place I am in, today. Not only did she offer state of the art genomic testing and interpretation, Dr. Kline provided dietary guidelines for me to follow and had samples of her dishes for me to try — so I could see how easy and delicious a healthier life could be. She gave me the most amazing recipes that she created in her own kitchen —many of which are now available in *The Blood Type Cookbook*. Life saver, Master Chef, best doctor ever…Thank you a million times over!"

- KIM GEDNEY

"Dr. Roberta Kline is skillful and compassionate healer. She is a true pioneer and has spent years learning and practicing in the fields of integrative and functional medicine where the science of lifestyle, genomics and epigenetics come together to provide a blueprint for the emerging field of personalized medicine known as nutrigenomics. Her knowledge and understanding of how the food we eat can interact with our genes to either promote health or create disease makes her the perfect candidate to share with us her recipes for wellness."

- GENE GRESH, R.PH., FIACP
Compounding Pharmacist/Functional
Medicine Practitioner

"I've known Bobbi Kline for many years and she has always impressed me with her culinary creativity. When our children were in school, we would meet for lunch. Lunch at my house would always be the same old thing—soup or peanut butter and jelly. But Bobbi always made something new and different; I never believed her when she said she just threw ingredients together, because the result was always something beyond ordinary: A delectable soup, or exquisite salad full of flavor and color. Dinner at Bobbi's house was never standard fare. With every dish, she brought out textures and flavors with unique combinations of herbs and spices, always accompanied by some wonderful sauce or side dish…I know Bobbi has written *The Blood Type Cookbook* with love, passion, and great

attention to what our bodies need to be vibrantly healthy. And, most importantly, I know each recipe will be delicious!

- CELESTE CUMMING

Special Praise from Dr. Kline's Daughters

"More often than not, kids complain about the food on the dinner table. My mom's always been an amazing cook and she makes healthy food taste delicious, no matter what it is. I highly recommend the Asparagus with Macadamia Nuts & Cherries. (How often do you hear a kid say that?) Moving out after high school will have one major drawback: I will no longer be able to eat her food whenever I want to!"

-MARISSA SOBANSKI
(Dr. Kline's youngest daughter)

"Eating has never been so rewarding with *The Blood Type Cookbook*! I'm quite lucky my mom is a doctor who practices what she preaches. She has put delectable dishes on the dinner table, quickly and easily all of my life. Now, she is bringing her healthy and delicious recipes to so many more people who may have thought life is too busy to prepare great-tasting meals. I have many favorite dishes from this cookbook, but I am absolutely obsessed with the Stuffed Acorn Squash and Turkey Wrap recipes—I think your family will be, too!"

-SELENA SOBANSKI
(Dr. Kline's eldest daughter)

ACKNOWLEDGEMENTS

As with any worthwhile endeavor, there are many people who have contributed in meaningful ways along my journey.

First, to the patients who have entrusted their health and wellbeing to my care. You have touched my soul with your courage to create meaningful, healthy change in your lives. You have my deepest gratitude.

In life and in medicine, I have been blessed with many teachers including **Dorothy Martin-Neville**, PhD, who introduced me to energy medicine and was instrumental in my own healing and personal growth. Also, **Priscilla Bengtson**, mentor, teacher, spiritual guide and friend—with your wisdom and support you showed me how to reconnect with my own inner vision and strength. **Kim Gedney**, my biggest cheerleader and the friend who never let me lose sight of the person I am and what I am here to do. My soul sister, you inspire me every day with your courage and strength.

Gene Gresh and Nicholas Palermo, you showed up when I needed colleagues who believed we could change medicine; you stayed and became friends. **Celeste Cumming**, you have walked many miles with me as we have gone through challenging years together. Thank you for your friendship.

Recipe testers extraordinaire, **Selena** and **Marissa**: your honest feedback helped improve my recipes—or sometimes just take them off the table! Thanks for all the encouragement and your help. And, for **Tucker.**

Karen M. Rider, your writing expertise, coaching and encouragement helped me envision how to turn a collection of recipes into a cookbook that anyone could use easily and creatively. Thank you for keeping the "i's dotted and the t's crossed!"

Books are indeed judged by their cover; thank you, **Shaila Abdullah** and her team at **My House of Design** for the beautiful cover design and for launching this cookbook into the world.

This cookbook could not have come together without **Joe Veltmann's** vision and encouragement. I am forever grateful that you chose to share with me your ideas, knowledge, and most of all your unconditional love and support.

INTRODUCTION

Are you looking to incorporate the principles of personalized nutrition based on your blood type into a simple, healthy eating plan that the whole family can enjoy? Do you find it challenging to prepare one meal for all the different blood types at your dinner table? In *The Blood Type Cookbook: Easy, Healthy and Delicious Recipes for the Whole Family*, I will show you how you can quickly create meals for all family members, regardless of their blood type and without hassle.

For most families, life is busy, time is short, and there are people of multiple blood types living under one roof. I created this cookbook out of a need to be able to put healthy, great tasting meals on the table that everyone in my family could eat. As a single working mom with a busy medical practice and two teenagers, dinner often is the only time that we all sit down for a meal together. It was difficult to remember who could eat what, and I found myself frustrated flipping through the guidelines for each blood type. Making several different dishes each night, resulting in more time preparing meals and more dirty dishes to clean, did not fit my belief that cooking delicious, healthy foods can be simple and easy. I needed easy-to-prepare recipes made with ingredients found in my local grocery stores. My solution was to create recipes using foods that all of us, regardless of blood type, could enjoy at the dinner table.

You might be wondering what made me, a women's health physician, choose The Blood Type Diet® in the first place. In the 20-plus years I have practiced medicine, I have used many different approaches to healthy eating with my patients as well as for my family and myself. Before I discovered The Blood Type Diet®, developed by naturopathic physician Dr. Peter D'Adamo, I had intuitively reduced most gluten and dairy products, noticing I felt better when I did. However, this did not

completely alleviate the bloating, gas, and discomfort that I had lived with all my life; symptoms chalked up to "irritable bowel syndrome." After only a few weeks of following the guidelines for my blood type, I noticed that my "good" days, which used to be infrequent, became the norm. Within a few months, I felt so much better—bloating occurred only when I did not follow the guidelines for my blood type. Many other symptoms that I had learned to endure—rosacea, fatigue, mood swings—were also greatly improved. Even through very stressful times, I noticed I was coping better. I decided it was time to introduce this way of eating to both my patients and to my daughters. As I applied the principles of the blood type diet with my family, we all noticed we felt more energetic and were healthier when we ate according to blood type.

Eating for Your Type
Why It Matters

It was clear to me The Blood Type Diet® was different in its approach to understanding how the body uses food for optimal health and wellbeing. At the heart of eating according to your blood type is the goal to increase foods that nurture and nourish the body, and decrease or eliminate those foods that can contribute to inflammation and illness. The theory behind The

Blood Type Diet® is that each blood type (O, A, B, AB), which is determined by your genes and influenced by ancestral origins, provides a genetic map for personalized nutrition that can improve your health, increase energy and reduce risk for chronic disease. Many independent researchers have linked blood type, diet and health but Dr. D'Adamo pioneered a comprehensive guide to eating according to blood type in his book *Eat Right 4 Your Type*. If you aren't familiar with the blood type diet, or need a simple refresher, I recommend reading his book.

You might find it interesting to know that eating according to your blood type—essentially eating according to your personal genetic needs—ties right into a new field of research on personalized nutrition called nutritional genomics (or nutrigenomics). Nutrigenomics is the study of how food affects our genes and how individual genetic differences can affect the way we respond to nutrients in the foods we eat. The tools of nutrigenomics include dietary approaches, lifestyle changes and nutritional supplements that optimize health and lower the risk for illness. Dr. Joe Veltmann, PhD, a nutritional biochemist and genomics expert, and my partner and cofounder at Genomic Solutions NOW!® LLC, has been using blood type dietary guidelines as an important component of personalized nutrition plans for his clients for many years. We are discovering how the nutrients and components of the foods we eat can affect us right down to our very core—our genes—with the potential to create health and healing or increase the potential for inflammation and disease.

The Doctor is in the Kitchen

Cooking has always been a passion, a creative outlet for me. I am an intuitive cook, creating dishes out of whatever I have on hand in my fridge and pantry, and getting them on the table in a short amount of time. As I experimented with recipes and received feedback from others (especially Dr. Joe), I realized I wanted to share my solutions with other people faced with the same challenge I had: how to easily prepare healthy and delicious meals using everyday ingredients that are acceptable for all blood types. My hope is *The Blood Type Cookbook: Easy, Healthy and Delicious Recipes for the Whole Family* helps you incorporate a variety of disease preventing and health enhancing foods into wonderful meals to be enjoyed by all family members.

Wishing you joyous eating and vibrant health,

Dr Bobbi

Dr. Bobbi

P.S. I am excited to bring this book to you, and I would love to hear how you are using it! Please join the Facebook community (http://facebook.com/genomicsolutionsnow.com) or connect on Twitter (http://twitter.com/GenomicSolution). Whichever way you prefer to connect, I'd love to know what you think about the recipes, and I invite you to share recipes you've created from the Shopping List included in this book.

HOW TO USE THIS COOKBOOK

I have organized The Blood Type Cookbook to make it easy for you to find the ingredients you need and the type of meal you want to serve. Additionally, I've included other resources to make your time spent in the grocery store and in the kitchen an easy, healthy and fun experience.

About the Recipes shows you how the recipes in this book are organized. It also highlights things for you to consider before making substitutions (such as for sweeteners or oils) in any of the recipes.

Dr. Bobbi's **Time Saving Prep Tips & Shopping Tips** include simple, cost-effective solutions for organizing your pantry, getting the most out of your grocery dollars and enhancing your health by purchasing the most nutrient dense, freshest foods you can afford.

The Grocery Shopping List was created especially for this cookbook. As I was creating recipes for my family, I quickly realized that I needed a list of foods that I could use, one that I could post on my fridge and take with me to the grocery store. Dr. Joe Veltmann graciously shared with me a list he had created for his patients, and it became an invaluable resource for me…and, I hope for you too. To download a printable shopping list, just scan the QR code on the back of this book, or go to www.genomicsolutionsnow.com/shopping-list/.

ABOUT THE RECIPES

The recipes are organized by meal. You can mix and match from any of the sections for an endless variety.

Many of the recipes in *The Blood Type Cookbook* can be made for breakfast, lunch, or dinner—feel free to mix-and-match meals to suit your preferences. **Great Beginnings** includes unique spins on more traditional breakfast foods to start your day. Two of my personal favorites are Squash Pancakes and Quinoa with Dried Fruit and Walnuts. **The Center Plate** contains recipes that are higher in protein and hearty enough for a dinner meal. My daughters love the Mahi-Mahi with Curry Sauce. **Sidelights** are just that—side dishes that you can pair with a main dish selection for a complete meal. Roasted Butternut Squash Bites are a big hit around my house. The recipes found in **Lite Bites** include soups and salads that can be served alone or in combination for a lighter meal. I think you'll love the Bibb Salad with Toasted Walnuts. Of course, no cookbook is complete without **Indulgent Endings** like Key Lime Pie with Toasted Almond Crust to satisfy that sweet tooth.

Several recipes are used with others included in this cookbook; these can be found in the **Little Extras** section. I often make these items to keep on hand: Prune Butter, Fig-Apricot Spread, Toasted Nuts, and Joe's Green Tea Tonic.

Substitutions within Recipes

Most everything in this cookbook is wheat and gluten-free. Where there are exceptions, I offer a substitution to make the recipe gluten-free. Otherwise, substitutions are generally acceptable, but there are a few caveats for you to keep in mind:

As with any dietary approach or recipe you wish to follow, be sure to consult with your personal healthcare provider (e.g., physician, nutritionist, etc.) to make sure the approach is right for you. If you have known allergies to any ingredient, use a substitute that is acceptable for your health needs. If you aren't sure about a substitution, consult with your healthcare provider. You also can post a question to the Facebook community page.

Milk substitutes—rice, almond, and hemp—should be fairly interchangeable. The taste and texture may vary, so personal preference will play a role.

Oils have a different flavor and temperature smoke point (the point at which the nutritional benefits decline and potentially harmful ones form). While they can be used interchangeably, the taste will be slightly different. While olive oil has a higher smoke point than flaxseed oil, neither should really be used at high temperatures.

I generally prefer olive oil. Feel free to try different oils and experiment with different tastes.

Butter, while it is dairy, is generally acceptable for all blood types. It can be used interchangeably with ghee, which is Indian clarified butter. For those with lactose sensitivity, or who want to avoid dairy, the ghee is a good alternative as it retains much of the flavor and cooking properties, but has no milk proteins or lactose. You can purchase ghee in the specialty section of your grocery or in a store that specializes in Indian foods. Alternately, you can make your own ghee using the recipe in the **Little Extras** section.

I have not yet found a good substitute for vanilla and almond extracts in baking. And, much to my daughter's dismay, there are no good solutions here for chocoholics. Perhaps, I will have figured this out by my next book. In the meantime we keep a small stash of high-quality dark chocolate for those chocolate emergencies!

I have eliminated processed sugars for all the recipes. Instead, I use honey, agave and maple syrup. These sweeteners can be substituted for each other in many recipes, but will result in a different taste, so experiment and see what you like best. (More about sweeteners can be found in the **Shopping Tips**).

Salt is an excellent seasoning, and choosing your salt is important. The only benefit to processed salt is that it has added iodine, an important nutrient that is often lacking in modern diets. I recommend real mineral salt, or sea salt. It has many important minerals, and when used in moderation is part of a healthy diet.

In many of the recipes, I give instructions for both nonstick and conventional cookware. While many of the Teflon-coated pans in the past were made with a toxic chemical that was released with high heat or damaged surfaces, some of the newer versions are being made without PFOA. Ceramic and silicone nonstick coatings are excellent and don't contain any of these toxins. Using nonstick cookware does make for easier cooking and cleanup, along with less need for cooking oil. Stainless steel is also a good choice, as is cast iron. I do not recommend cooking with aluminum or copper cookware, as these metals can be linked to health issues.

DR. BOBBI'S
TIME SAVING PREP TIPS

Dr. Bobbi's Time Saving Prep Tips include simple, cost-effective solutions for organizing your pantry, getting the most out of your grocery dollars and enhancing your health by purchasing the most nutrient dense, freshest foods you can afford.

My number one time saving tip is to have the **Grocery Shopping List** handy when you are cooking and making trips to the grocery store. I keep one copy on my fridge and one copy in my purse.

Second, organize your herbs and spices. After several months of pulling out herbs and spices from my cabinet while cooking, only to realize that not all were okay for all blood types, I separated out those that everyone could use. I keep these on one shelf, or off to one side of a shelf. Other herbs and spices I labeled according to blood type. Especially when using the common spices such as cinnamon, nutmeg, clove and allspice, labels made it easy to have them handy to sprinkle on foods right at the dinner table, and know who could use what!

Third, organize your fridge and pantry. Take an inventory of the foods in your pantry and fridge now; if you find items that are not on the list set them aside. Try making room on a shelf for food for each individual blood type in your household, and label the shelves accordingly. This makes it easy to identify who can eat what for snacks or individual meals. The foods that are okay for all family members go front and center.

Fourth, keep a ready supply of prepared staple dishes. Side dishes, such as veggies and grains can be made in advance so they are readily available for use with other recipes during the week. I often make a batch of cooked brown rice or quinoa in the beginning of the week. This way, my Type A daughter can easily add grains to her meal, and I don't have to cook it separately each time.

DR. BOBBI'S SHOPPING TIPS

I hope you find these tips helpful and your shopping is made simpler. Above all, enjoy what you eat!

Organic, fresh or frozen fruits and vegetables have the highest levels of nutrients with lowest levels of chemicals. Berries in particular have very high levels of pesticides when grown conventionally. Canned produce has the lowest nutritional value, and often has added sugar and/or salt.

Canned foods, while generally less expensive, typically contain the chemical BPA in the lining. This chemical is linked to health problems because it interferes with your normal hormone system. Look for cans that say "BPA free," or limit to no more than 2 canned foods per week.

Buy wild caught fish whenever possible. Farmed fish can have higher levels of contaminants. Fish should not have a strong odor if it is fresh (frozen fish, when defrosted, likewise should not have a strong odor).

As often as possible, buy organic, free-range animal products: meat, poultry, eggs and dairy. Many animals are fed GMO corn, which should also be avoided if possible.

When purchasing oils, look for organic, cold-pressed versions. Avoid oils that have been heat-processed, as this destroys some of the healthy nutrients.

Beans are best and least expensive when purchased dried and in bulk. Preparation is not difficult, but it does mean you have to plan ahead to soak them. Canned beans are good to keep on hand for when you are short on time, and can be used in any of these recipes.

Select fresh-squeezed or 100% juice, without any added sugar. When you cook fresh cranberries in water, the juice can be saved for use in drinks or other recipes.

When buying prepared foods, read labels carefully, as there are often hidden ingredients. Corn and other grains as well as sugar can often be found in most packaged foods, particularly in gluten-free items. If these items are one of the first few in the ingredients list, leave it on the shelf and look for another product. If these ingredients are closer to last on the list, the small quantities will likely not affect you as long as you don't eat them frequently.

Special Tips for Sugar and Sugar Substitutes

Sugar in general is not healthy for any of us, whether it comes from table sugars or the other sweeteners listed here. Substituting other sweeteners still needs to be done in moderation.

Agave is very sweet, so use less when substituting it for sugar in your drinks and foods. There are several varieties (light, amber, dark); experiment to see which you like the best.

Maple syrup is also available in different grades. I prefer grade B, as that has a stronger maple taste and is slightly less sweet than the fancy grade A. It is also often less expensive, and now readily available in most stores. Honey is best when it is locally grown. It is not advised to feed raw honey to children less than one year of age.

Tips for Choosing Protein Powder and other Supplements

When choosing protein powder, look for one made from a combination of brown rice and pea proteins (preferably organic, non-GMO)-this give you a more complete supply of amino acids than just the rice alone. Whey protein is derived from milk and should only be used by those with B or AB blood type. Soy protein can be used by O's, A's, and AB's.

The VM 2525, Greens First and Ribozip supplements in the Protein Smoothie can be ordered from our website (http://www.genomicsolutionsnow.com/).

EmergenC can be found in any local drugstore.

THE BLOOD TYPE COOKBOOK GROCERY SHOPPING LIST

The foods on this shopping list are acceptable for all blood types.

Vegetables

- [ ] Acorn Squash
- [ ] Arugula
- [ ] Asparagus
- [ ] Bamboo Shoots
- [ ] Beets
- [ ] Beet Greens
- [ ] Bibb Lettuce
- [ ] Bok Choy
- [ ] Broccoli
- [ ] Butternut Squash
- [ ] Carrots
- [ ] Celery
- [ ] Collard Greens
- [ ] Cucumber
- [ ] Dandelion Greens
- [ ] Endive
- [ ] Garlic
- [ ] Kale
- [ ] Leek
- [ ] Okra
- [ ] Onions
  (red, yellow)
- [ ] Parsnips
- [ ] Romaine Lettuce
- [ ] Scallions
- [ ] Shallots
- [ ] Spinach
- [ ] Squash
- [ ] Swiss Chard
- [ ] Water Chestnuts
- [ ] Watercress
- [ ] Zucchini

Beans

- [ ] Cannellini Beans
- [ ] Green Peas
- [ ] Northern Beans
- [ ] Snap Beans
- [ ] Snow Peas
- [ ] White Beans

Fruits

- [ ] Apples
- [ ] Apricots
- [ ] Blueberries
- [ ] Boysenberries
- [ ] Cherries
- [ ] Cranberries
- [ ] Currants
- [ ] Dates
- [ ] Elderberries
- [ ] Figs
- [ ] Gooseberries
- [ ] Grapefruit
- [ ] Limes
- [ ] Lemons
- [ ] Nectarines
- [ ] Peaches
- [ ] Pears
- [ ] Pineapple
- [ ] Plums
- [ ] Prunes
- [ ] Raisins
- [ ] Raspberries

Nuts & Seeds

- [ ] Almonds
- [ ] Almond Butter
- [ ] Chestnuts
- [ ] Hickory Nuts
- [ ] Macadamia Nuts
- [ ] Walnuts

Grains

- [ ] Brown Rice
- [ ] Quinoa
- [ ] Spelt (faro)

Oils

☐ Flaxseed
☐ Olive

Fish & Seafood

☐ Cod
☐ Grouper
☐ Mahi-Mahi
☐ Monkfish
☐ Perch
☐ Red Snapper
☐ Salmon
☐ Trout
☐ Tuna

Meat & Poultry

☐ Turkey
☐ Eggs

Dairy & Nondairy Substitutes

☐ Almond Yogurt
☐ Greek Almond Yogurt
☐ Butter/Ghee
☐ Farmers Cheese
☐ Feta Cheese
☐ Goat Cheese
☐ Mozzarella

☐ Rice Cheese
☐ Almond Milk
☐ Hemp Milk
☐ Rice Milk

Cereals

☐ Cream of Rice
☐ Ezekiel Flakes
☐ Puffed Rice
☐ Rice Bran

Breads

☐ Almond
☐ Brown Rice
☐ Ezekiel

Herbs & Spices

☐ Agar
☐ Arrowroot
☐ Basil
☐ Bay Leaf
☐ Bergamot
☐ Cardamom
☐ Carob
☐ Chives
☐ Chocolate
☐ Coriander
☐ Cream of Tartar
☐ Cumin

☐ Curry
☐ Dill
☐ Dulse flakes
☐ Garlic
☐ Kelp
☐ Lowry's salt
☐ Marjoram
☐ Mint
☐ Paprika
☐ Parsley
☐ Saffron
☐ Sage
☐ Sea Salt
☐ Savory
☐ Spearmint
☐ Tamari
☐ Tarragon
☐ Thyme
☐ Turmeric

Spices

Specific to your blood type
☐ O: allspice
☐ A: cinnamon
☐ B: nutmeg
☐ AB: cinnamon

Sweeteners

☐ Agave
☐ Brown Rice Syrup
☐ Honey
☐ Maple Syrup
☐ Molasses

Juices

☐ Apricot
☐ Black Cherry
☐ Carrot
☐ Celery
☐ Cranberry
☐ Grapefruit
☐ Lemon
☐ Lime
☐ Pineapple
☐ Prune

Herbal Teas

☐ Green
☐ Ginger
☐ Peppermint
☐ Rosehips

Miscellaneous

☐ Red Wine

ABOUT THE AUTHORS

Roberta L. Kline, M.D.

Roberta Kline, M.D. is passionate about empowering others with the knowledge and tools they need to create health of mind, body and spirit. She feels deeply that our health is intimately connected to the foods we eat and to the lifestyle we create for ourselves physically, emotionally, energetically and spiritually. Eating based on blood type is one of the cornerstones of her personalized medicine and functional genomics consulting practice.

Board-certified in obstetrics and gynecology, with additional training in functional medicine, genomics, and multiple healing modalities, "Dr. Bobbi" actively shares her knowledge and vision through writing, teaching and speaking. She has created curricula for teaching medical residents and master's degree students the principles of functional medicine,

energy medicine, genomics and epigenetics. Dr. Bobbi is cofounder and CEO of Genomic Solutions NOW!® LLC, dedicated to teaching others how to create individualized health based on one's genes. She also serves as Assistant Clinical Professor at the University of New England College of Osteopathic Medicine, and Guest Faculty Instructor for The Graduate Institute in Connecticut.

When she isn't seeing patients, teaching or conducting research, Dr. Bobbi is usually in the kitchen, experimenting with new flavors, textures and creative ways to present delicious meals for busy families. Her other favorite past times include hiking, playing piano and guitar, and travel to exotic destinations.

Joe R. Veltmann Ph.D.
FAAIM, DCCN

Joe R. Veltmann, PhD has over thirty years experience as a nutritional research scientist, and twenty-five years as a nutritional, functional and integrative medicine practitioner. For more than a decade, Joe has helped his patients understand the inter-relationship between genes, internal and external environments, nutritional and dietary habits, and lifestyle choices in the prevention and treatment of chronic diseases, including cancer. As part of his personalized medicine practice, Dr. Joe has been using The Blood Type Diet® with his patients with great success. In 2005, Joe was certified as a Fellow and Master Instructor in Dr. Peter D'Adamo's Institute for Human Individuality.

When the human genome project was completed in 2000, Joe was one of the first to delve into genomic testing and interpretation, and its application to improving health. As founder of the GENESIS Center for Integrative Medicine, he created a personalized medicine and healing model based on genetic predispositions, environment, nutrition, exercise, stress, inflammation and spirituality. His passion to help healthcare practitioners bring genomics to personalized medicine led to his role as Chief Science Officer for Estrogen Gene, LLC, as well as Co-founder and CSO for Genomic Solutions NOW!® LLC. An international consultant and speaker, Joe trains healthcare practitioners and teaches individuals from around the world how to create better health through personalized, functional genomic medicine.

Dr. Joe enjoys hiking and playing with his dog, Tai, in addition to swimming, traveling, and creating delicious ways to make dishes more nutritious.

Extraordinary Blueberry Muffins

GREAT BEGINNINGS

Breakfast

PROTEIN SUPER SMOOTHIE

I never liked protein smoothies until Joe Veltmann showed me his secret recipe using his special green tea, and lots of it. The sweetness of the tea, plus the additional liquid, makes for a great start to my day without the grittiness typical of protein shakes. Be sure to use a spoon to get all the good fiber if it settles to the bottom of the glass.

Place all ingredients in a blender.

Pulse blend for about 10 seconds. Pour into large glass or mug.

🥄 DR. BOBBI'S PREP TIPS:

If using frozen fruit, let it defrost first for a thinner drink. I will often let the frozen fruit soak with the green tea tonic in the blender for a few minutes, and that does the trick!

Remember, it is best to use a combined pea and brown rice protein powder.

Feel free to experiment and add other fruits and veggies from the shopping list; some of our favorites are baby carrots, slices of lemon and lime, baby spinach and cucumber. You can also use leftovers from recipes in this book: Apple Crumble, Honey Baked Carrots, Baked Squash or Simple Sweet Greens.

Serves 1 (3 cups)

*VM 2525 powder, RiboZip, and Greens First are supplements you can find at the Genomic Solutions NOW!® website. EmergenC is available at drugstores. The dose of VM 2525 powder is most accurate when based on your individual genes.

Ingredients

3 cups Joe's Green Tea Tonic (see recipe p. 78)
½ cup mixed fruit (any combination of fresh or frozen blueberries, nectarines, peaches, boysenberries, apples, cherries, pineapple, plums, cranberries or raspberries)
2 scoops protein powder*
1-2 tsp. VM 2525 powder*
1 packet EmergenC* (I love the blueberry acai, but choose your favorite)
1 scoop RiboZip*
1 scoop Greens First*

GOAT CHEESE, SPINACH & EGG WRAP

*A great way to eat healthy on the go (yes, we all have those days)!
You can use only egg whites if you prefer. The spinach should be
just lightly wilted; if it is cooked too much it creates a soggy wrap.*

Whisk eggs or egg whites in a bowl and set aside.

Preheat saucepan over low-medium heat, and spray with olive oil spray (for nonstick pan), or use 1 Tbsp. olive oil.

Sauté onions and pears until soft, about 7 minutes. Push the mixture to the side of the pan. Add eggs to pan; scramble, stirring gently, until cooked through. Add the spinach leaves, cover, and cook until slightly wilted, about 2 minutes.

Salt to taste.

Meanwhile, reheat the tortilla according to package directions (easier to fold when heated). Place the egg and spinach mixture into the center, top with turkey bacon and either goat or mozzarella cheese. Fold the ends of the tortilla over the mixture, roll up & enjoy!

Ingredients

*2 eggs or 3 egg whites
¼ pear, diced
⅛ cup red onion, diced
1 cup baby spinach
1 strip cooked turkey bacon
1 oz. goat cheese or mozzarella cheese, cut into small pieces
Olive oil
⅛ tsp. salt, to taste
Ezekiel or brown rice tortilla wrap*

EXTRAORDINARY BLUEBERRY MUFFINS

Almond flour adds texture, protein and sweetness to these gluten-free muffins. You can substitute raisins, currants, dried or fresh cranberries for the blueberries if you wish. These freeze well, and I often make extra to stash in the freezer for those days when I don't have time to make breakfast.

Preheat oven to 350°F. Line standard muffin tin with 12 baking cups.

Mix dry ingredients together in a bowl.

In a separate bowl, whisk eggs. Add oil and honey, whisk again. Mix in the blueberries.

Add the dry ingredients to the wet and mix well.

Fill baking cups about ⅔ full. Bake for 18–22 minutes. Let stand a few minutes in the muffin tin before removing to cooling rack. Be sure muffins are cooled completely before placing in storage container.

Ingredients

2 cups almond flour
1 cup brown rice flour
1 tsp. baking soda
½ tsp. baking powder
¼ tsp. salt
2 Tbsp. light olive oil
½ cup honey
3 eggs
1 cup fresh or frozen blueberries

QUINOA WITH DRIED FRUIT & WALNUTS

This hearty meal is a good substitute for traditional hot cereals such as oatmeal, cream of wheat or grits. I often serve this as a delicious hot breakfast in the winter months. It's equally satisfying served cold as the weather warms. Experiment with other dried and fresh fruits on the Shopping List.

Place all ingredients except dates and walnuts in a 3 qt. pot, cook over high heat until it boils. Reduce heat to low, cover, and simmer 10 minutes, or until all liquid is absorbed. Add nuts and dates; fluff with a fork and serve hot or cold.

DR. BOBBI'S PREP TIPS:

Try pan-frying refrigerated leftovers and serving with honey, agave, or maple syrup.

Add a dash of spice appropriate for your blood type just before serving:

O: Allspice
A: Cinnamon
B: Nutmeg
AB: Cinnamon

Serves 4

Ingredients

2 cups dried quinoa, rinsed and drained
(this removes any bitterness)
3 ¾ cups water
½ cup 100% apricot juice, unsweetened
½ cup dates, chopped
½ cup currants
½ cup mission figs, chopped
¾ cup walnuts, chopped

SPINACH OMELET

This is one of my favorite ways to create an omelet and it's easiest in a nonstick pan. Even if you don't have one, the key is to have the pan and oil hot enough before adding the eggs, and then covering the pan while cooking the greens.

Preheat skillet over medium heat; spray with oil if nonstick, otherwise add 1 Tbsp. oil to pan. Sauté shallots for 3 minutes.

While shallots are cooking, whisk eggs together in a bowl, then whisk in salt. Add eggs and swirl pan to form even layer on the bottom.

Cook, undisturbed for 1 minute. Sprinkle the feta cheese over the eggs, and then add the spinach.

Cover, cook another 2 minutes, or until spinach is just wilted. Fold the omelet in half on itself; transfer to plate to serve.

Serves 1

Ingredients

2 Tbsp. thinly sliced shallots
1 Tbsp. olive oil or spray
2 eggs
dash salt
pinch marjoram
1 cup baby spinach
1 Tbsp. crumbled feta cheese

SQUASH PANCAKES

When a lazy Sunday morning calls for pancakes, these hit the spot. Using a store-bought gluten-free pancake mix makes it easy, and adding the protein and squash boosts the nutritional value. Just be sure to read the label on the mix—look for brown rice flour as the main ingredient, with no corn.

Preheat griddle to 375°F.

Whisk together eggs in a large bowl. Add the squash, almond milk, water, and oil and mix well.

In a separate bowl, combine the pancake mix, baking soda and protein powder. Add to the wet ingredients and mix well. Stir in the walnuts.

Lightly oil the griddle with light olive oil. Using a ⅓ cup measure for each pancake, pour batter onto hot griddle. (If you prefer smaller pancakes, use a ¼ cup measure).

Cook for 2-3 minutes; when bubbles form on the top, the bottom will be golden brown. Flip pancakes; cook another 1-2 minutes until bottom golden brown.

Keep warm until ready to serve.

Serve plain, or add honey, agave, or maple syrup and enjoy!

🥄 DR. BOBBI'S PREP TIPS:

Pumpkin can be substituted for the squash if you are O, A, and AB.

*I use the King Arthur brand

Serves 4-6

Ingredients

1 package (15 oz.) gluten-free pancake mix*
2 eggs
2 cups almond milk
¼ cup packed canned squash (such as butternut)
1 Tbsp. water
4 Tbsp. light olive oil
1 tsp. baking soda
1 scoop protein powder (brown rice and pea)
½ cup chopped walnuts

BAKED EGG & ZUCCHINI "QUICHE"

I have reworked one of my favorite dishes here. Not only does it taste great hot or cold, it is much easier to prepare and so much healthier than typical quiche recipes! Enjoy the leftovers for lunch or even dinner, the next day. To make this recipe gluten-free, substitute brown rice bread for the Ezekiel bread.

Preheat oven to 375°F.

Beat 8 eggs in a large bowl until light and fluffy; add the salt, dill and tarragon.

In a separate bowl, whisk together rice milk and arrowroot powder. Add to egg mixture and whisk to mix. Stir in leeks and zucchini.

Arrange the Ezekiel bread halves on the bottom of a 9x12 glass baking pan. Pour the egg and vegetable mixture evenly over the bread. Top with feta cheese.

Bake for 40 minutes, or until a knife inserted into the center comes out clean.

Serves 6

Ingredients

8 eggs
¾ tsp. salt
½ tsp. dill weed
½ tsp. dried tarragon
3 cups unsweetened rice milk
2 Tbsp. arrowroot powder
4 slices Ezekiel bread, cut in half
1 large leek (white part only), cut lengthwise
  and sliced thinly
2 medium zucchini, cut lengthwise and sliced thinly
½ cup crumbled feta cheese

Curried Turkey with Greens

THE CENTER PLATE

Main Dishes

MAHI-MAHI WITH CURRY SAUCE

You can use a mild or hot curry spice, depending on your preference. This recipe can be used with any mild fish—cod, monkfish, red snapper or grouper.

Place the pears and apricots in a bowl, add the curry powder and mix well. Add the water and honey, mix.

Preheat a large saucepan over medium heat; add olive oil (or spray with oil spray if nonstick pan).

Place Mahi-Mahi filets in the pan and cook for 4-5 minutes. Turn filets over and add the fruit mixture to the pan. Cover; simmer over low-medium heat for 10 minutes. Fish should flake with a fork.

Serve fish topped with the curry sauce.

🍴 DR. BOBBI'S PREP TIPS:

Serve with brown rice and steamed or sautéed greens such as the Simple Sweet Greens (see recipe p. 87).

Serves 4

Ingredients

1 lb. Mahi-Mahi filet, cut into four equal pieces
1 pear, cored and diced
12 dried apricots, diced
1 Tbsp. curry powder
½ cup water
1 Tbsp. honey
1 Tbsp. of olive oil (if using nonstick pan, use olive oil spray)

CURRIED TURKEY WITH GREENS

A sweet and spicy way to cook the greens, I love this dish and so do my girls. The curry is given extra depth and contrast by an unexpected combination of fig, apricot, and squash.

Make a paste of the Fig-Apricot Spread, squash, almonds, water and 1 Tbsp. curry. Set aside.

Preheat large skillet over medium-low heat; add 1 Tbsp. olive oil (or spray bottom if nonstick pan). Add turkey cutlets, sprinkle tops with ½ Tbsp. curry powder, and cook 5-7 minutes depending on thickness, until bottom is browned. Turn slices over, sprinkle tops with another ½ Tbsp. curry powder, and cook through, about another 5 minutes. Remove from pan and keep warm.

Add 1 Tbsp. olive oil to pan, or spray with olive oil spray, and add pears and leeks; cover and cook 5 minutes, stirring frequently. Add the greens, cover, and cook 4 minutes (the greens will be just wilted). Stir the fig-apricot mixture into the greens and heat through.

Divide the greens onto four plates. Top each with a turkey cutlet and serve.

Serves 4

Ingredients

4 turkey cutlets, about 4 oz. each
3 cups coarsely chopped collard greens
3 cups coarsely chopped Swiss chard
2 cups baby spinach
1 large or 2 small leeks, ends trimmed; thinly sliced
2 pears, cored and cut into 1-inch chunks
2 Tbsp. curry powder
¼ cup Fig-Apricot Spread (see recipe p. 74)
¼ cup packed squash
¼ cup water
¼ cup toasted slivered or sliced almonds
Olive oil or spray

TROUT WITH MAPLE-ALMOND BUTTER

A simple and elegant way to serve trout. Prepare the butter up to 1 day ahead to save time. This is delicious served with brown rice and Honey Baked Carrots.

Prepare Maple-Almond Butter:

Mix first 4 ingredients in a small bowl, blend well. If preparing ahead of time, refrigerate overnight, and bring to room temperature before preparing the fish.

Prepare fish:

Preheat broiler. Lightly coat baking sheet with light olive oil spray. Place trout skin side down on baking sheet. Brush olive oil over trout. Broil until fish is opaque in the center, about 4-6 minutes. Remove from oven.

Transfer fish to plates; sprinkle with parsley. Top with a small pat of the maple-almond butter and serve.

Serves 4

Ingredients

3 Tbsp. butter (or ghee), room temperature
¼ cup toasted sliced almonds
4 tsp. maple syrup
1 Tbsp. lemon juice
4 trout, boned
2 Tbsp. olive oil
light olive oil spray
2 Tbsp. fresh parsley (or 1 Tbsp. dried)

PESTO PASTA WITH VEGETABLES

We just love the fresh flavor of pesto, and this version meets The Blood Type Diet® guidelines while retaining the delicious flavor! Feel free to adjust the garlic to taste. You can add cannellini beans or peas for extra nutrition, and the kids will never be the wiser! If you cook the veggies with the pasta, you'll have a one-pot meal ready in less than 20 minutes. What could be better?

Place garlic in food processor and mince. Add basil leaves, purée until smooth, about 1 minute. Scrape sides if needed. Add walnuts and purée until smooth. Add lemon juice, and drizzle olive oil from the top while puréeing mixture until pesto is uniform texture. If you like your pesto thinner, add olive oil as above to taste in 1 Tbsp. increments.

Boil water for pasta. Add pasta and frozen vegetables, stir and reduce heat to med-high; cook pasta per package directions. Drain. Return pasta and vegetables to pot. Add the pesto and mix well. Serve.

✖ DR. BOBBI'S PREP TIPS:

For added protein, you can keep this dish vegan by adding ¼ cup cannellini beans and 1 Tbsp. olive oil to the pesto after you have puréed the walnuts. Even easier, use the Bean Pâté (see recipe p. 84).

Another alternative is to toss cut-up cooked turkey in with the pasta and veggies.

*When purchasing gluten-free pasta, look carefully for corn or other grains; you want to use brands that have only brown rice and/or quinoa.

Serves 4

Ingredients

3 cups tightly packed fresh basil leaves (about 4 oz.)
2 large or 3 medium garlic cloves
1 cup toasted walnuts
½ cup olive oil
1 Tbsp. lemon juice
¼ tsp. salt
4 cups frozen vegetables (any combination of broccoli florets, peas, carrots)
4 cups dry gluten-free pasta (brown rice or quinoa)*
water

SEARED TUNA WITH SPINACH SALAD

Deceptively simple, the flavors blend beautifully in this dinner salad. The red Steamed Beets used in this recipe need to be done ahead of time so they can chill. I often make a larger batch and store in the fridge for multiple uses. You can cook the tuna ahead of time and serve it cold, but I love the contrast of the warm tuna with the cold salad.

Combine the honey, olive oil, lemon juice, cumin and red onion in a small bowl. Set aside.

Wash and drain the spinach leaves, divide evenly between 4 plates. Top spinach with beets and peaches.

Combine salt and paprika in a small bowl, set aside.

Preheat skillet over medium heat; add butter and melt. Place tuna filets in pan; sprinkle the tops with half of the salt mixture. Cover and cook 5 minutes; they should be nicely browned on the bottom. Turn the tuna filets over, sprinkle with the remaining salt mixture. Cover, and cook another for another 3-5 minutes. The tuna should flake easily with a fork, and the middle should be just pink. Remove from heat.

Top the prepared salad plates with the tuna filets. Drizzle with dressing to taste.

Serves 4

Ingredients

1 ½ cups red Steamed Beets, chilled and cut up into 1-inch chunks (see recipe p. 51)
2 peaches or nectarines, pitted, cut into 1-inch pieces
6 cups baby spinach
4 tuna fillets, approximately 4 ounces each
2 tsp. butter or ghee
½ tsp. salt
½ tsp. paprika

Dressing

¼ cup honey
¼ cup olive oil
¼ cup lemon juice
4 Tbsp. diced red onion
dash cumin

HERB ROASTED TURKEY & VEGETABLES

A delicious meal when you have time to plan ahead. The herb rub gives the turkey a savory taste and smells heavenly when it is roasting! The olive oil keeps the meat moist. Prep time is minimal, no need to peel the carrots or apples. I use the leftover turkey to make a delicious turkey soup.

Preheat oven to 350⁰F. Mix the herbs together in a small bowl, then add ithe olive oil and mix well.

Place the turkey in a large roasting pan. Carefully separate the skin over the breast with your fingers, as far as you can go. Then, spread half of the herb rub between the skin and the breast. Spread the remainder over the entire surface of the turkey.

Mix the vegetables and fruit in a large bowl; place in the pan, around the turkey. Pour ½ cup of the broth or water over the vegetables. Roast turkey about 15 min. for each pound, or until the juices run clear.

Every half hour or so, during roasting, stir the vegetable mixture and baste the turkey with remaining broth or water (and wine if desired). Remove from oven when turkey is done.

Let rest 10 min. prior to carving. Serve with roasted vegetables and juices.

Serves 6-8 with leftovers

Ingredients

8–10 lb. whole turkey
6 carrots, washed and cut into 2- inch pieces
2 medium onions cut into 2-inch pieces
2 tart cooking apples, cored and cut into 2-inch pieces
8 oz. pitted prunes
1 cup turkey broth or water
¼ cup red wine, optional

Herb rub

½ tsp. salt
1 tsp. dried tarragon
1 tsp. thyme
½ tsp. dried sage
½ tsp. dried savory
2 Tbsp. olive oil

SALMON WITH DILL SAUCE

An easy way to prepare salmon, the olive oil keeps the fish moist while broiling. By cutting the filet into four pieces, the cooking time is reduced and dinner is on the table in less than 20 minutes.

Preheat broiler.

Lightly grease baking sheet with olive oil. Place salmon filet on sheet, skin side down.

Prepare Dill Sauce:

In a small bowl, whisk together the olive oil, Tamari, dill and lemon juice. Brush evenly over the salmon.

Broil 8-10 minutes, or until the center is cooked through and flakes with a fork.

Enjoy this dish along with Asparagus with Macadamia Nuts and Dried Cherries (see recipe p. 44).

Serves 4

Ingredients

1 lb. wild salmon filet, cut into four pieces
2 Tbsp. olive oil
1 tsp. dried dill weed
1 Tbsp. lemon juice
1 tsp. Tamari

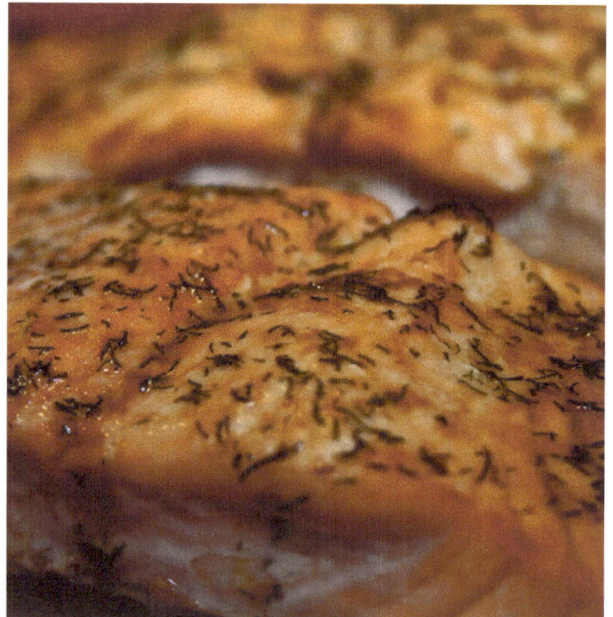

MACADAMIA NUT-CRUSTED BAKED COD

The macadamia nuts add a surprising sweetness to this light dish. Cutting the fish filet into individual portions makes preparation easier and lets you get dinner on the table in less than 30 minutes!

Preheat oven to 400°F.

Line shallow baking pan or cookie sheet with parchment paper.

In a shallow bowl, whisk together eggs, rice milk and salt.

In a food processor, coarsely grind nuts. Place in a separate shallow bowl.

Dip cod filet into the egg mixture, then thickly coat with the nut mixture. Place on prepared baking sheet. Repeat with the remaining filets.

Bake 15-20 minutes, depending on thickness, or until fish flakes with fork.

Enjoy this dish with Roasted Butternut Squash Bites (see recipe p. 47) or Roasted Vegetables (see recipe p. 53).

Serves 4

Ingredients

1 pound cod filet, cut into 4 equal pieces
½ cup macadamia nuts
½ cup raw almond slivers
2 eggs
2 Tbsp. rice milk
¼ tsp. salt

TURKEY WITH COLLARD GREENS & RICE

This is a hearty meal, great for those cold fall or winter days. The sweetness from the fruit provides a palate pleasing contrast to the typically bitter collard greens.

In a large nonstick saucepan, brown the ground turkey; about 10 minutes. Add the salt, collard greens, paprika, coriander, ¼ cup water, figs and walnuts and cover to steam until the greens are wilted, about 5-7 minutes. Mix the prune butter and ¼ cup water in a small bowl; add to the turkey and greens mixture and stir to combine.

While the greens are cooking, place the warm brown rice into a bowl, and stir in the goat or feta cheese. Let the cheese soften slightly.

Divide the brown rice mixture evenly between four plates. Spoon the turkey mixture over the rice and serve.

Top individual servings with spices appropriate for blood type:

O: Allspice
A: Cinnamon
B: Nutmeg
AB: Cinnamon

Serves 4

Ingredients

1 pound ground turkey
½ tsp. salt
8 cups coarsely chopped collard greens
½ cup chopped dried figs
½ cup walnuts, coarsely chopped
¼ cup Prune Butter (see recipe p. 81)
4 cups cooked brown rice, warmed
½ cup diced goat or feta cheese
water

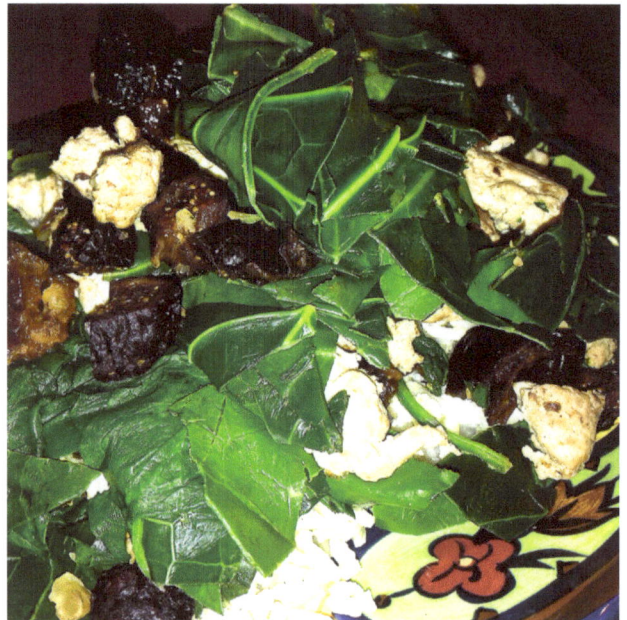

STUFFED SQUASH

A recipe from one of my favorite cookbooks, *The Moosewood Cookbook*, inspired this recipe. I have revamped it to fit the blood type diet guidelines, and it is just as delicious.

Preheat oven to 400°F. Lightly grease the bottom of a baking pan or a cookie sheet.

Remove seeds and stringy portion of acorn squash with a spoon. Place the squash cut-side down. Bake for 30-40 minutes, until squash is tender. Turn oven off, flip the squash over and keep warm.

Melt butter in nonstick saucepan over medium heat, stir in the olive oil. Sauté the onions, apples, raisins and walnuts until the onions are clear and soft, about 7 minutes. Stir in coriander, mix well. Stir in the goat cheese. Cover and cook for another 3 minutes, or until the cheese has softened.

Scoop the apple mixture into the acorn squash halves.

Sprinkle with blood-type appropriate spices just before serving:

O: Allspice

A: Cinnamon

B: Nutmeg

AB: Cinnamon

Serves 4

Ingredients

2 acorn squash, split length-wise in half
½ cup chopped Vidalia or other sweet onion
2 medium apples, cored and chopped
½ cup raisins or currants
½ cup coarsely chopped walnuts
1 Tbsp. butter or ghee
1 Tbsp. olive oil
3 oz. goat cheese, diced into ½ inch cubes
1 tsp. coriander

THE BLOOD TYPE COOKBOOK

QUICK SALMON WITH GREENS

When the fresh fish isn't available, canned salmon makes for a great and economical way to eat this healthy fish. Paired with the scallions and lemon dill dressing, this simple and delectable dinner salad can be put together in minutes.

Toss the greens and snow peas together. Divide evenly among four plates.

Remove the salmon from the can. Use a fork to break into large chunks, and divide into four portions. Place one portion salmon onto each plate of greens. Sprinkle the scallions on top.

Prepare Dressing:
Whisk together the dressing ingredients.

Drizzle over salads, to taste. Serve and enjoy.

Serves 4

Ingredients

1 15 -16 oz. can wild salmon
3 cups coarsely shredded romaine lettuce
3 cups arugula and/or baby spinach
4 scallions, roots trimmed; sliced into ½-inch
   pieces (use green part too)
1 cup snow peas

Lemon dill dressing

⅓ cup lemon juice
¼ cup olive oil
¼ cup water
2 tsp. dried dill
pinch salt

42

Simple Sweet Greens

SIDELIGHTS

Veggies & Grains

ASPARAGUS WITH MACADAMIA NUTS & CHERRIES

Simple and elegant. The asparagus is best when still crisp. The dried cherries add a colorful contrast to the asparagus, along with healthy polyphenols.

Preheat nonstick skillet over medium heat, melt butter and stir in olive oil; heat through. Add the nuts, and sauté until just starting to brown, about 2 minutes.

Add the cherries, then the asparagus stalks. Add the water and a dash of salt; cover; and cook for 3-5 minutes, depending on the thickness of the asparagus. It will be bright green and crisp-tender.

Remove asparagus from pan, top with the cherries and nuts. Serve immediately.

Serves 4

Ingredients

1 pound asparagus stalks, washed and trimmed
¼ cup coarsely chopped macadamia nuts
¼ cup dried cherries
½ Tbsp. olive oil
1 tsp. butter or ghee
2 Tbsp. water
dash salt

HONEY BAKED CARROTS

A simple and delicious way to prepare carrots, this is
a family favorite. I like them still a little crunchy;
cook longer if you prefer more tender carrots.

Preheat oven to 400°F.

Place carrots and water in a large casserole dish.
Combine the honey and butter, stir in the salt and
coriander; drizzle over carrots.

Bake, covered, for 30 minutes for crunchier carrots; 45
minutes for softer carrots.

**Sprinkle with blood-type appropriate spices just
before serving:**

O: Allspice

A: Cinnamon

B: Nutmeg

AB: Cinnamon

Serves 4

Ingredients

*16 medium carrots, washed and cut into 2-inch pieces
(to save time, you can substitute one 32 oz. bag of baby
carrots)*

½ cup water

½ cup honey

1 Tbsp. butter or ghee, melted

½ tsp. salt

½ tsp. coriander

STEAMED BROCCOLI WITH CHERRIES & FETA

This is a far cry from plain steamed broccoli. The contrast of textures, colors and tastes creates a dish worthy of taking center stage at your table. To make this into a meal, just add turkey and top it over brown rice.

Place broccoli and cherries in steamer; cook until broccoli turns bright green and is crisp-tender, about 8 minutes.

Transfer to serving bowl. Add feta cheese, wait 1-2 minutes to let the cheese melt slightly.

Add the nuts and stir to mix. Serve and enjoy.

Serves 4

Ingredients

4 cups broccoli florets cut into 2-inch chunks (frozen broccoli florets work just as well)
½ cup crumbled feta cheese
½ cup sliced almonds
½ cup coarsely chopped walnuts
½ cup dried cherries

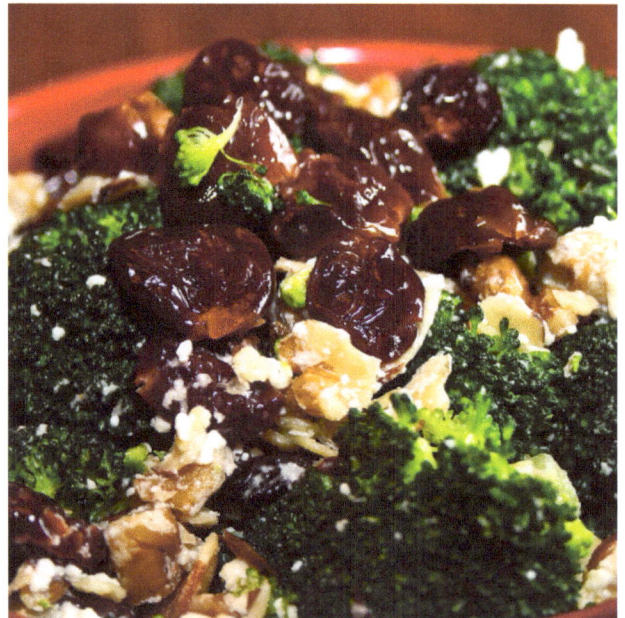

ROASTED BUTTERNUT SQUASH BITES

For years, this was the only way my daughters would eat squash. The sugars in the squash caramelize as it cooks, adding crunch and sweetness. The squash is delicious on its own, and leftovers can be added to soups or grains. To make it easy to prepare, I often buy the squash already peeled and cut.

Preheat oven to 425°F.

Place squash pieces on cookie sheet. Drizzle with the olive oil, and toss to coat. Spread out on pan so there is an even layer. Sprinkle with sea salt.

Bake for 20 minutes. Bottoms of the squash will be browned and crispy, while the squash will be soft. Serve warm.

Serves 4

Ingredients

4 cups butternut squash pieces, about 1-inch size
1 Tbsp. olive oil
1 tsp. coarse sea salt

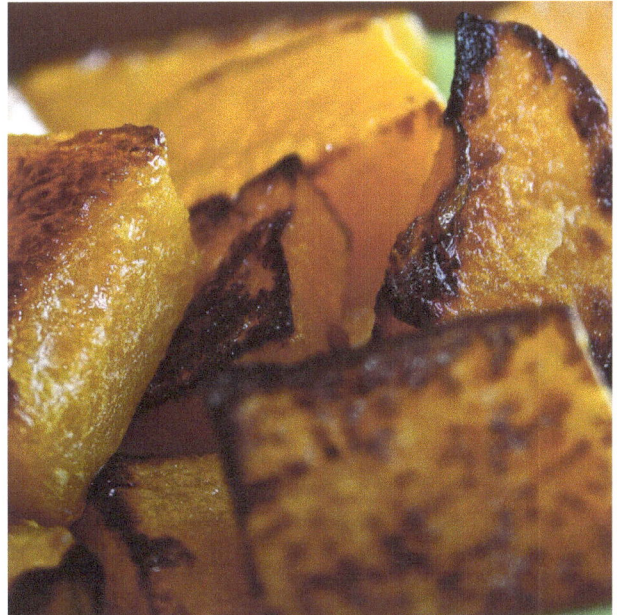

FRIED BROWN RICE

A fast and healthy version of a family favorite. It makes a great option for a hot breakfast, and a terrific way to use up miscellaneous leftover vegetables hanging out in the fridge or freezer.

Preheat large skillet, add 1 Tbsp. olive oil; or spray bottom if nonstick.

Add the rice, stir to heat through. Make a clearing in the middle and pour the eggs into this space. Cook, stirring eggs frequently. Stir to combine the cooked eggs and rice.

Add the vegetables, and sauté until heated through and crisp-tender. Sprinkle mozzarella cheese and mix lightly.

Serve with tamari sauce to taste.

Serves 4

Ingredients

3 cups cooked brown rice
3 eggs, lightly beaten (you can substitute 4 egg whites)
4 cups diced vegetables (any combination of broccoli, carrots, onions, bamboo shoots, water chestnuts, celery, bok choy, watercress)
¼ cup shredded mozzarella
1 Tbsp olive oil, or olive oil spray
Tamari sauce to taste

ZUCCHINI MEDLEY

The northern beans add protein and contrast to the vegetables. This dish is terrific hot or cold. Try serving over brown rice to make it a light meal.

Preheat large skillet over medium heat; add olive oil (or lightly spray with olive oil if using nonstick pan).

Sauté onions 5 minutes, stirring frequently. Add zucchini, cover and cook another 5 minutes, stirring occasionally. Add the peas, northern beans, herbs and salt; stir.

Cover; cook 5 minutes, stirring occasionally.

☒ DR. BOBBI'S PREP TIPS:

Serve over brown rice to make this a complete meal.

For variation, add a dash of tamari sauce, or serve cold with a sprinkle of lime juice.

Serves 4

Ingredients

4 medium zucchini, cut into 1-inch pieces
½ red onion, diced
1 cup canned northern beans, rinsed and drained
1 cup frozen peas
1 tsp. dried tarragon
1 tsp. dried parsley
½ tsp. salt
½ tsp. paprika
1 Tbsp. olive oil or olive oil spray

ROASTED SQUASH WITH CRANBERRIES

This is a great way to serve squash, combining sweet and sour tastes. It is worthy of the finest table!

Preheat oven to 400°F. Lightly spray bottom of glass baking pan with light olive oil.

Cut squash in half lengthwise, forming 4 halves. Remove the seeds and stringy portion with a spoon. Place cut-side down in the baking pan and bake about 50 minutes, or until squash is fork-tender.

While the squash is cooking, prepare the filling. Combined the apple, water (or juice), walnuts, maple syrup and cranberries in a saucepan. Cook over medium heat until it is simmering, about 10 minutes. Reduce heat to low and cook another 10 minutes, or until apples are tender. Keep warm until the squash is done.

Remove squash from oven. Turn halves over. Fill squash halves evenly with the filling. Serve warm.

Serves 4

Ingredients

2 medium acorn squash
1 large apple, peeled, cored and diced
light olive oil
½ cup chopped walnuts
¼ cup maple syrup
¼ cup water
½ cup fresh or dried cranberries (if using dried cranberries, substitute unsweetened cranberry juice for the water)

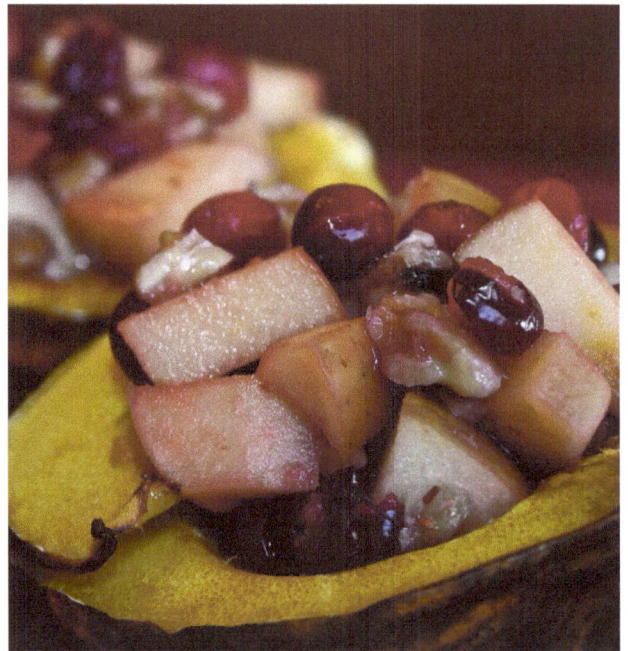

STEAMED BEETS

These are so simple, sweet and delicious, you'll never go back to canned beets! No need to peel them—they are soft and tender as is. You can use any color beets. I recommend cooking red beets separately as the color will stain the others if cooked together. I like to make extra to keep on hand in the fridge to add to salads or cooked greens, or even a smoothie in the morning.

Cut beets into 1-2 inch pieces. Place in steamer basket, add water to the pot to just below the beets in the basket. Cover and bring to a boil. Reduce heat and cook, covered, until beets are soft to a fork, about 8-10 minutes.

Serve warm or cold.

❦ DR. BOBBI'S PREP TIPS:

Store the leftover cooking water in the fridge, and add it to your smoothie for color, sweetness, and added nutritional value.

In the waste not, want not department. Do not throw out the beet green tops, they can substitute for Swiss Chard in the Blood Type Cookbook Recipes.

Serves 4

Ingredients

6 large or 9 medium beets, greens removed, trimmed and scrubbed
Water

SIMPLE SWEET GREENS

An easy way to get your greens in! The pears and cranberries add a sweet contrast. I often will eat leftovers for breakfast, served over quinoa or as a side dish with eggs.

Prepare sauté pan over medium-low heat; add 1 Tbsp. olive oil (or spray bottom of pan if using nonstick). Sauté pears, onions and cranberries for 10 minutes, stirring frequently.

Add ¼ cup of water, Prune Butter, salt and coriander and stir. Add the chopped greens, cover and cook 5 minutes, or until greens are wilted. Stir to combine.

Delicious as is, or serve topped with a sprinkle of your choice of spice.

Sprinkle with blood-type appropriate spices just before serving:

O: Allspice or Clove
A: Cinnamon or Allspice
B: Nutmeg or Clove
AB: Nutmeg or Clove

Serves 4-6

Ingredients

½ Vidalia or sweet onion, chopped
2 pears, cored and cut into 1-inch pieces
8 cups mixed greens, coarsely chopped (choose several for best results: beet greens, Swiss chard, baby spinach, dandelion greens, collard greens, kale)
2 Tbsp. Prune Butter (see recipe p. 81)
1 Tbsp. light olive oil
1 ½ cups fresh cranberries (or 3/4 cup dried)
¼ tsp. salt
¼ tsp. coriander
¼ cup water

ROASTED VEGETABLES

Ah, this is pure comfort food in the fall and winter. It takes a little longer to cook, but so worth the wait! For those of you who can eat sweet potatoes (sorry blood type A's), these work great as well.

Preheat oven to 425°F.

Place veggies and fruit in a 3-qt or 8x10 glass baking dish.

In a small bowl, mix the liquid ingredients; add in the cardamom, coriander and cumin. Pour over the vegetable mixture and stir to coat. Bake for 45 minutes, stirring occasionally.

✴ DR. BOBBI'S PREP TIPS:

O's, B's and AB's can eat sweet potatoes, and these are terrific in this recipe as well. You can add in 1 medium sweet potato, cut into 1-inch chunks, to the recipe, and bake in a 9x12 glass pan.

Serves 4-6

Ingredients

*6 large or 8 medium yellow beets, trimmed,
    scrubbed, and cut up into 1-inch chunks*
1 large red onion cut into 1-inch chunks
1 cup prunes
½ cup dried cherries
¼ cup honey
1 Tbsp. olive oil
½ cup water
1 tsp. lemon juice
¼ tsp. cardamom
½ tsp. coriander
Dash of cumin

Turkey Soup

LITE BITES
Salads, Soups & Wraps

BROWN RICE & SPINACH SALAD

Joe's creation that combines the rice and feta cheese is oh so yummy! It turns an ordinary spinach salad into a tasty, hearty meal with the unexpected combination of hot and cold.

Add the feta cheese to hot rice, stir to mix until cheese slightly melted.

Place spinach on top of rice mixture. Top with the scallions, cranberries, and cucumber.

Prepare Dressing:
Whisk the olive oil and lemon juice in a bowl. Add water and a pinch of salt. Whisk to combine.

Lightly pour over salad and serve.

DR. BOBBI'S PREP TIPS:
Try making this with arugula instead of spinach for a different flavor.

Serves 4

Ingredients

2 cups brown rice, cooked
½ cup crumbled feta cheese
2 scallions, roots trimmed and thinly sliced (include the green part)
½ cup dried cranberries or cherries
1 cucumber, peeled; sliced lengthwise into quarters, then sliced into ½-inch pieces
4 cups baby spinach

Lemon and olive oil dressing

¼ cup olive oil
¼ cup lemon juice
3 Tbsp. water
pinch salt

ELEGANT ENDIVE & GOAT CHEESE

This dish is elegant and rich. Endives provide a beautiful canvas for the cheese and fig spread. A light lunch all on its own, or a lovely accompaniment to your favorite soup or salad.

Wash and pat dry endive leaves.

In a bowl, blend the cheese and 4 Tbsp. rice milk until slightly stiff spreading consistency. Add another 1 Tbsp. rice milk if needed. Mix in the apples and ½ cup of walnuts.

Divide the Fig-Apricot Spread evenly among the endive leaves—gently spread along the lower, thicker part of the leaves. Carefully spread the goat cheese mixture over the Fig-Apricot. Sprinkle with scallions and remaining walnuts. Serve.

🥄 DR. BOBBI'S PREP TIPS:
Substitute celery sticks for the endive (you'll need about 8 large stalks), and you have a great party snack, or a handy finger-food version for the younger (and young-at-heart) folks in your family.

Serves 4

Ingredients
8 large or 16 small endive leaves
1 apple, such as McIntosh, Cortland, or Pink Lady, cored and diced
4 ounces goat cheese, softened
4-5 Tbsp. rice milk
½ cup Fig-Apricot Spread (see recipe p. 79)
½ cup chopped walnuts, plus 2 Tbsp. for garnish
1 Tbsp. sliced scallions

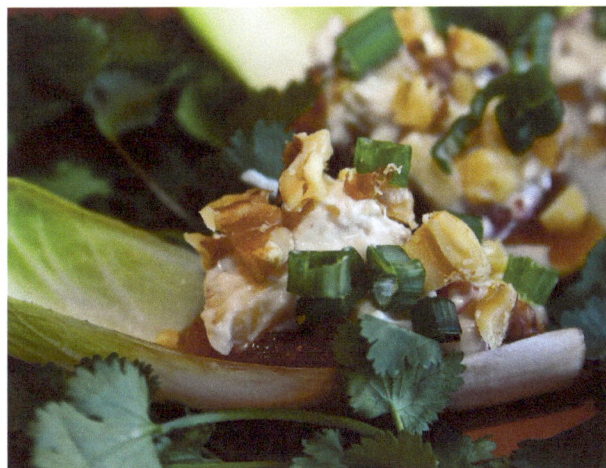

CANNELLINI BEAN & WALNUT SALAD

This is a light salad, with the beans and nuts providing a good source of protein. The kale is a beautiful backdrop for the salad. Perfect for a spring lunch!

Gently mix the first four ingredients in a bowl.

In a smaller bowl, whisk together the garlic, salt, oil, lemon juice and herbs. Pour over the bean mixture; gently toss to coat.

Trim ends from kale; place one leaf on each plate. Top the kale with the bean mixture, dividing evenly. Sprinkle lightly with the dulse flakes if desired, and serve.

Serves 4

Ingredients

1 can (15 oz.) cannellini beans
1 red onion, cut into quarters then thinly sliced
1 English cucumber, peeled, cut in half lengthwise, and sliced ½-inch thick
½ cup walnut pieces
2 cloves garlic, crushed
¼ tsp. salt
¼ cup olive oil
¼ cup lemon juice
1 tsp. tarragon
1 tsp. parsley
4 kale leaves
1 Tbsp. dulse flakes (kelp or seaweed flakes), optional

BIBB SALAD WITH TOASTED WALNUTS

Toasting the walnuts creates a deeper flavor, and it's so easy to do.
This salad is light and sweet. If it's available at your grocer, red kale
provides a beautiful contrast to the cucumber and Bibb lettuce.

Place lettuce in a large bowl. Arrange the kale around the outer edge of the lettuce.

Place dressing ingredients in a bowl and whisk until well combined. Add the toasted walnuts, apples, celery, cucumber and cherries; stir to combine well.

Place the above mixture on top of the lettuce. Top with the feta cheese if desired.

Serves 4 main dishes; 6-8 side dishes

Ingredients

6 cups washed and coarsely torn Bibb lettuce
3 cups coarsely chopped kale
1 cup toasted walnuts (see recipe p. 80)
2 apples, cored and chopped
2 stalks celery, thickly sliced (½-inch)
1 English cucumber, peeled, halved lengthwise and sliced
½ cup dried cherries
2 Tbsp. finely crumbled feta cheese, optional

Dressing

¼ cup lime juice
¼ cup olive oil
1 Tbsp. maple syrup
¼ cup chilled raspberry tea

VEGETABLE BROTH

One challenge to store-bought vegetable broth is that it often contains vegetables that are not good for all blood types. If you find one that works, keep some on hand. Otherwise, here is one you can make yourself. Feel free to freeze for later use.

Place all ingredients in a large pot. Cover and bring to a boil. Simmer, covered, 1-3 hours (the longer you simmer, the more concentrated the flavors become).

Remove the vegetables with a slotted spoon.

Refrigerate or freeze until ready to use.

Makes 8 cups

Ingredients

10 cups water
2 large onions, skins on, cut in half
½ leek, trimmed and cut in half lengthwise
6 stalks celery, washed, cut in half (include greens)
3 carrots, cut in half
1 tsp. salt
1 tsp. dried tarragon
1 tsp. dried basil
½ tsp. dried marjoram

TURKEY BROTH

As with the vegetable broth, you can buy pre-made turkey broth or make your own. The availability of turkey broth can vary with the store and time of year, so if it's an item not readily available to you, plan ahead and make a large batch and freeze for later.

Place all ingredients in a large pot. Cover and bring to a boil. Simmer, covered, 1-3 hours (the longer you simmer, the more concentrated the flavors become).

Remove all vegetables and the carcass.

Strain the broth if desired; I prefer mine unstrained, as the herbs will continue to season the broth.

Refrigerate or freeze until ready to use.

Makes 8 cups

Ingredients

10 cups water
Carcass from an 8-10 lb. turkey, meat removed, plus any drippings
2 large onions, skins on, cut in half
3 carrots, cut in half
3 stalks celery, cut in half (include greens)
1 apple, cored and cut in half
1 tsp. salt
1 tsp. dried thyme
1 tsp. dried savory
½ tsp. dried sage
2 bay leaves

SPLIT PEA SOUP

The turkey bacon adds a great smoky flavor to this hearty soup, but you can make it without for a vegan dish. This is even better the next day; you may need to add more water when reheating, as it tends to thicken overnight.

In a large pot, heat the olive oil over medium heat. Add the turkey bacon and onion. Sauté 10 minutes, or until the bacon bits are browned and the onion is translucent.

Add the remaining ingredients, stir.

Cover and cook over medium-high heat until it comes to a boil. Reduce heat to medium low and simmer, covered, stirring occasionally for 45 minutes.

Uncover, cook another 15 minutes, stirring occasionally, or until most of liquid is absorbed. Soup will be thick.

Serves 8

Ingredients

1 16-oz package dried split peas
8 strips turkey bacon, diced
1 onion, diced
6 carrots, washed and sliced about ¼ inch thick
1 bay leaf
1 tsp. salt
1 tsp. tarragon
8 cups water
½ tsp. coriander
1 Tbsp. olive oil

TURKEY SOUP

This is a great way to use the leftover roast turkey to make a delicious soup. Eat it fresh or freeze portions to enjoy later.

Put the turkey in a large pot; add the remaining ingredients except for the spinach. Bring to a boil, then cover and reduce heat to med-low; simmer 45 min–1 hour, or until the carrots and squash are fork-tender. Add salt to taste.

Remove the turkey carcass to a large cutting board. Check for any loose bones or large pieces of meat in the soup and remove these with a slotted spoon. Discard the bones and cut up the meat into bite-sized pieces.

Add the meat back to the pot. Salt to taste.

Add the spinach, cook another 3-5 minutes until wilted; serve.

Serves 8

Ingredients

Leftover herbed 6-8 lb. roast turkey carcass, with some meat, plus any leftover liquid
8 cups water
3 ribs celery, with leaves, sliced ½ inch thick
3 carrots, sliced ½ inch thick
3 cups baby spinach
1 cup butternut squash, cut into 1-inch pieces
1 bay leaf
¼ tsp. dried sage
¼ tsp. dried tarragon
¼ tsp. dried savory
¼ tsp. coriander
Salt to taste

BUTTERNUT SQUASH SOUP

This is one of our favorites. For fast and easy preparation, I will buy fresh or frozen squash that is already peeled and cut into chunks. Adding the spices at the end adds depth while keeping to the blood type principles.

Melt butter or ghee in a large pot over medium heat, stir in olive oil and heat through. Add onion and sauté until onion is softened and clear, about 5 minutes. Add squash, apple, and 4 cups turkey or vegetable broth. Bring to a boil, then reduce heat and simmer covered until squash and apples are softened, about 30 minutes. Add more broth if needed to keep liquid just covering the apples and squash.

Using immersion blender, puree the ingredients in the pot. (If you do not have an immersion blender, puree in a food processor or blender.) Add more broth if needed for desired consistency. Add the maple syrup and stir.

Ladle soup into bowls.

Garnish with a dollop of almond yogurt if desired.

Sprinkle with blood-type appropriate spices just before serving:

O: Allspice

A: Cinnamon

B: Nutmeg

AB: Cinnamon

Serves 4

Ingredients

4 cups of cut-up butternut squash (about 1-inch size pieces)

½ large sweet onion, diced

4-5 cups vegetable or turkey broth (see recipe p. 60 or p. 61)

2 sweet apples, such as McIntosh, peeled, cored and diced

1 Tbsp. maple syrup

½ Tbsp. butter or ghee

½ Tbsp. olive oil

Non-dairy rice or almond yogurt for garnish, if desired

VEGETABLE SOUP

The secret ingredient is to use leftover Butternut Squash Soup. (If you don't have it on hand, feel free to use store bought butternut squash soup). It adds a sweetness and depth, without overpowering the vegetables.

In a large saucepan, heat the oil over medium heat. Add leeks, and sauté for 5 minutes. Add carrots, sauté another 5 minutes.

Add the vegetable broth, butternut squash soup, coriander and salt; cover and simmer 30 minutes.

Stir in the beans and Swiss chard. Cover, and cook until the Swiss chard is just wilted.

Sprinkle with the parsley and serve.

Serves 4

Ingredients

4 cups vegetable broth (see recipe p. 60)
½ cup butternut squash soup (see recipe p. 64)
1 16-oz can cannellini beans
4 medium carrots, washed and sliced about ¼ inch thick
1 leek, washed, ends trimmed, and sliced about ¼ inch thick
3 large leaves rainbow Swiss chard, coarsely chopped
1 Tbsp. olive oil
1 tsp. dried parsley
½ tsp. salt
½ tsp. coriander

SOUP
IN A HURRY

For times when you need something fast but still want it to be healthy, think about using canned soup as a quick starting point. You may need to add more liquid—water, vegetable or turkey broth—to your liking. Look for ones that are made with organic ingredients and no extra additives, if you can.

First, select your canned (or boxed) soup, and place it in the saucepan. Don't stress if some of the smaller ingredients aren't on your blood type list; remember it's about the big picture.

Then, jazz it up by adding fresh or frozen veggies, simmer until heated through, and you've transformed a ho-hum meal into one that tastes great and is packed with nutrition.

Some ideas for soups generally okay for all blood types:

Roasted turkey with vegetables
Vegetable soup (avoid soups with a tomato base)
Butternut Squash Soup
Cannellini or Northern Bean Soup

Vegetables you can add

Peas
Butternut squash chunks or puree
Chopped Swiss chard
Chopped or baby spinach
Sliced okra
Diced carrots
Diced celery
Cannellini beans
Broccoli florets
Zucchini
Snow peas

Grains you can add

Cooked brown rice
Cooked quinoa

Meats you can add

Cooked turkey, cut up
Cooked Turkey Bacon, chopped

TURKEY & APRICOT WRAP

A great way to use leftover roasted turkey, you can heat the wrap before
adding the lettuce for a luscious, melt-in-your-mouth sensation.

Spread the Fig-Apricot Spread in the middle of the wrap;
top with cheese.

Sprinkle walnuts over the spread and cheese, then place
the turkey over the mixture.

If you prefer a hot wrap, heat at this point on a nonstick
skillet or in the microwave.

Top with the lettuce. Fold the ends over, roll it
up, enjoy!

Serves 1

Ingredients

1 Ezekiel or brown rice tortilla
3 oz. turkey breast slices
1 oz. goat cheese, sliced into 3 pieces
2 Tbsp. Fig-Apricot Spread (see recipe p. 79)
1 Tbsp. chopped walnuts
½ cup shredded romaine lettuce

CURRIED TUNA WRAP

I love curry, and this is a fun twist on the usual tuna sandwich. I generally don't need much additional moisture when I use the tuna in olive oil, but you can add the almond yogurt to your taste. The brown rice wraps tend to crack more easily than their flour-based cousins; heating is recommended to make rolling them easier.

Place drained tuna in a bowl, flake with fork into small chunks. Add 2 Tbsp. almond yogurt and curry powder; mix well. This mixture is fairly dry; add almond yogurt if you prefer it more moist.

Add the apple, currants and celery, mix to coat.

Heat wrap according to package directions.

Spread 1 Tbsp. Fig-Apricot Spread on each wrap. Place ¼ of the tuna mixture in the center of each wrap; top each with ½ cup lettuce. Fold over ends, roll it up and enjoy!

Serves 4

Ingredients

2 cans albacore tuna, drained
2-4 Tbsp. Greek-style almond yogurt
1 Tbsp. curry powder
1 apple, cored and diced
1 large or 2 small stalks celery, diced
¾ cup currants or raisins
4 Tbsp. Fig-Apricot Spread (see recipe p. 79)
2 cups shredded romaine lettuce
4 Ezekiel or brown rice wraps

INDULGENT ENDINGS

Desserts for Your Sweet Tooth

KEY LIME PIE WITH TOASTED ALMOND CRUST

This is one of my favorite pies, and the inspiration for the addition of chocolate comes from Godiva's decadent key lime truffles. That's a treat clearly not on my blood type diet; this pie lets me indulge without the guilt!

Preheat oven to 350°F.

Coarsely grind almonds in food processor. Place in bowl and stir in salt. Mix in the butter with a fork until even texture. Stir in the agave and chocolate chips.

Use fork dipped in cold water to press the mixture evenly along the bottom and sides of 8-inch pie dish; it will be thick. Bake for 10 minutes. Cool completely.

Whisk the eggs, then add the rest of the ingredients and whisk until well blended. Pour mixture (it will be thin) into cooled nut crust. Bake for 35 minutes or until center is just set. Cool before serving.

*I use Enjoy Life brand

Serves 8

Crust

2 ½ cups toasted slivered or sliced almonds (see recipe p. 80)
¼ tsp. salt
4 Tbsp. softened butter or ghee
1 Tbsp. agave
*½ cup mini soy and dairy free chocolate chips**

Filling

½ cup key lime juice
8 -10 Tbsp. agave (10 if you like your key lime pie sweeter)
1 ½ Tbsp. arrowroot powder
3 eggs
1 cup rice milk

APPLE CRUMBLE

Simple and sweet, this is my version of a classic dessert. For added indulgence, you can add a scoop of nondairy rice-milk ice cream, although I love it just as is.

Preheat oven to 375°F.

Place all fruit in a 3-qt casserole dish.

In a separate bowl, mix the lemon juice, honey, maple syrup and water. Pour over the fruit and toss gently to coat.

Mix together the almond flour, almonds and butter in a small bowl until the texture is even. With a pastry cutter (you can also use a fork), cut in the butter until the mixture is crumbly and uniform. Sprinkle evenly over the fruit mixture.

Bake for 30 minutes.

Sprinkle with blood-type appropriate spices just before serving:

A & AB: Cinnamon
B: Nutmeg
O: Allspice

Serves 4

Ingredients

3 apples, diced
16 dates, chopped
1 cup frozen (or fresh) dark cherries
2 Tbsp. lemon juice
2 Tbsp. honey
2 Tbsp. maple syrup (I prefer grade B)
4 Tbsp. water

Topping

¾ cup almond flour
½ cup coarsely ground almonds
3 Tbsp. softened butter or ghee

BERRY YOGURT PIE WITH MAPLE WALNUT CRUST

Almond yogurt combined with the berries creates a creamy, luscious pie that is good for you, too! This pie is even better after it sits overnight and the berry flavors deepen. I love the crust so much I will eat it by itself. Try this pie for breakfast—who says you can't start your day with dessert sometimes!

Preheat oven to 350°F.

Mix the walnuts, butter and maple syrup together in a bowl. Using a fork dipped in cold water spread the mixture evenly along bottom and sides of an 8-inch pie dish. Crust will be slightly thick. Bake for 10 minutes; cool completely.

Purée cranberries and raspberries in food processor or blender. Add remaining ingredients; blend well. Mixture will be consistency of cooked pudding.

Spread evenly into cooled maple walnut crust. Chill at least one hour before serving. Best when chilled in fridge overnight. Top with fresh raspberries if desired.

✗ DR. BOBBI'S PREP TIPS:

Don't have time to chill the pie for hours? Put it in the freezer for 15 minutes; it will be firm enough to serve. For a fun, quick alternative: Crumble the baked, cooled crust. Layer the filling and crust pieces in a parfait glass or large serving bowl. Top with fresh raspberries and serve.

Serves 8

Ingredients

24 ounces Greek-style almond yogurt
2 Tbsp. lime juice
2 Tbsp. agave
½ cup cooked cranberries, drained
1 cup fresh or frozen raspberries (if using frozen, defrost and drain juices)
1 Tbsp. arrowroot powder
Fresh raspberries for garnish if desired

Crust

2 cups coarsely ground walnuts
4 Tbsp. softened butter or ghee
4 Tbsp. Maple syrup

BROWN RICE PUDDING

This is comfort food, pure and simple. A sweet and satisfying dessert, I prefer it hot, although it is delicious cold too. You can serve it as a special breakfast treat, or use as a base for a curried vegetable dish.

Place rice, raisins and 2 cups of almond milk in a saucepan. Cover, and bring to a gentle boil over medium-high heat. Stir. Reduce heat to low, simmer covered 50 minutes.

Add the remaining almond milk and coriander, stir. Simmer covered another 30 minutes, stirring occasionally, or until all the liquid is absorbed. Stir in the maple syrup.

Pour small serving dishes (or large bowl). Serve warm.

Serves 4

Ingredients

1 cup short-grain brown rice
3 cups almond milk
½ cup raisins or currants
¼ tsp. coriander
⅛ cup maple syrup

BAKED MAPLE APPLES

Here is a very simple and delicious dish, a light and sweet dessert made from classic New England foods: apples and maple syrup. Best eaten right from the oven.

Preheat oven to 350°F.

Core apples. Brush insides with lemon juice. Place apples in glass baking dish.

Fill the inside of each apple with currants. Pour syrup over currants in apples. Add water to baking dish.

Bake for 45 minutes, occasionally spooning syrup mixture over apples.

Serve warm, and top apples with any remaining mixture from the pan.

Sprinkle with blood-type appropriate spices just before serving:
O: Allspice
A & AB: Cinnamon
B: Nutmeg

Serves 4

Ingredients

4 apples (Rome or Cortland are best, but any firm cooking apple will do)
1 ½ Tbsp. lemon juice
1 cup currants or raisins
½ cup maple syrup
¼ cup water

GRILLED PINEAPPLE

These are so sweet made with freshly picked fruit, as the sugar caramelizes on the grill. For best results and healthiest grilling, use a gas grill on medium to prevent charbroiling. You don't want them to be burned. This also works well with nectarines, peaches and plums. If you don't have a gas grill, or there's a foot of snow outside, you can make these in the broiler too.

Preheat gas grill to medium. Lightly spray cut sides of fruit with oil (this keeps it from sticking to the grill). Place pineapple on grill.

Cook for about 5 minutes, or until the fruit is slightly soft and has nicely browned (but not black) grill marks. Turn pineapple over and repeat on the other side.

Serve immediately.

DR. BOBBI'S PREP TIPS:

If grilling the peaches, nectarines, or plums, grill cut side only, for about 8 minutes or until the fruit is slightly soft and has nicely browned grill marks.

Serves 4

Ingredients

One whole fresh pineapple, peeled, cored and cut lengthwise into spears
-or-
8 nectarines or peaches, cut lengthwise in half and pits removed
-or-
8 plums, cut lengthwise in half and pits removed

Olive oil spray

FIG COMPOTE

This is definitely an adult dish. Very rich, a little goes a long way. Delicious by itself, even better with non-dairy almond yogurt or rice milk ice cream.

Place all ingredients in saucepan. Cover; bring to boil over med-high heat. Reduce heat to low, and simmer, covered, 45 minutes.

Uncover and simmer for 15 minutes longer. The mixture should be fairly thick, with most of the liquid absorbed.

Serve hot or cold, excellent served on top of nondairy almond yogurt, rice milk ice cream, or goat cheese.

Serves 4

Ingredients

2 10-oz packages Turkish figs, stems removed and cut in half
4 thin slices lemon, seeds removed
¼ cup honey
½ tsp. coriander
1 Tbsp. agave
1 cup water
½ cup tart cherry juice
1 cup red wine, best to use full-bodied and slightly sweet type such as Syrah, Merlot, Carménère

THE LITTLE EXTRAS

JOE'S GREEN TEA TONIC

This is a delicious way to get in your green tea plus your fiber. Joe and I like to leave the loose tea leaves in with the liquid, but feel free to remove after steeping. Sip tea throughout the day, add to your smoothies, and even use it instead of water for your salad dressing.

Boil water. Pour into large heatproof glass or stainless steel pitcher or pot.

Remove paper tags from green tea bags, if present. Add the green tea bags and the fruit tea (loose or bags) to the water.

Cover; let sit for 1 hour. Remove tea bags. Remove loose tea leaves, if desired.

🍴 DR. BOBBI'S PREP TIPS:

If you are lucky enough to live in a sunny climate, you can put the pitcher or pot with the teas outside to make sun tea. Let it soak for at least 4 hours in direct sunlight.

The variations are endless- try adding lemon or lime slices, cooked cranberries, pineapple or other fruits from the grocery list after steeping the tea.

Makes 16 cups

Ingredients

16 cups filtered water
9 bags green tea
¼ cup loose leaf fruit tea – or – 5 fruit tea bags, choose from: boysenberry, elderberry, peach, cranberry, blueberry, cherry, guava, raspberry

FIG-APRICOT SPREAD

This slightly sweet spread can be used on toast, crackers, wraps, or as an addition to any curry dish, even on fish or turkey. I use an immersion blender here, which is easier and makes for much faster cleanup than using a food processor.

Place figs, apricots, and water in a saucepan and bring to a boil. Reduce heat to low and cover. Simmer 45 minutes. The fruit should be very soft, and a small amount liquid will be left in the pan.

Use an immersion blender to puree the Fig-Apricot mixture until smooth. Add a small amount of additional water if needed; the mixture should be very thick. Add agave and blend.

Spoon into a 2-cup container. Store in the fridge.

✗ DR. BOBBI'S PREP TIPS:

I love my immersion blender, as it minimizes prep time and saves on cleanup. If you don't have one, you can use a food processor or a blender that can handle thick mixtures.

Makes 2 cups

Ingredients

10 oz. dried Turkish figs, stems removed (approximately 2 ½ cups)
10 oz. dried apricots (approximately 2 ½ cups)
½ tsp. coriander
2 cups water
1 Tbsp. agave

TOASTED NUTS

Toasted nuts are so easy to make, and the flavors can make such a difference in a recipe! The basic technique is the same for any nut. Here I use it with walnuts and almonds, both good for all blood types. Feel free to double the batch and store in an airtight container so you always have some on hand.

Preheat oven to 350°F.

Spread nuts in even layer on a baking sheet.

Bake for 8 minutes, stirring occasionally until nuts are slightly browned and fragrant. Cool.

Use immediately, or store in airtight container.

Makes 1 cup toasted nuts

Ingredients

1 cup sliced or slivered almonds, or walnut halves or pieces

PRUNE BUTTER

This is deliciously sweet all by itself, and can be used in many ways. Try it anywhere you would use jam. It is a wonderful topping for meats, and creates magic with sautéed greens.

Place prunes and water in a saucepan; heat to boiling. Cover and reduce heat to low. Simmer for 30 minutes. The prunes should be soft, and only a small amount of liquid left in the pan.

Puree using an immersion blender or food processor. Add a small amount of additional water if needed; this mixture should be thick.

Transfer prune butter into a 1 cup container and refrigerate.

Makes 1 cups

Ingredients

10 oz. prunes
1 cup water

COOKED CRANBERRIES

These are delicious and have so many uses: add to greens, smoothies, or eat them on their own- hot or cold. Add some of the leftover juice to water for a lighter cranberry juice drink. Try replacing cranberry sauce with this healthier alternative next Thanksgiving.

Place cranberries in saucepan; add enough water to just cover the cranberries (when they just start to float). Cover and bring to gentle boil over medium-high heat.

Reduce to low; simmer until berries just start to split open, about 5-7 minutes.

Use right away, or store in the juices for up to a week in the fridge.

Serve with a sprinkle of spices (according to blood type) if desired:

O: Allspice

A: Cinnamon

B: Nutmeg

A & AB: Cinnamon

Makes 3 cups

Ingredients

16 oz. bag of fresh or frozen cranberries
water

LIME DRESSING WITH VARIATIONS

As vinegar is not good for any of the blood types, one of the first questions I am often asked is what to do for salad dressing. Lime juice is a great substitution for vinegar in salad dressings and marinades. Here are several ideas--feel free to experiment and create your own dressing variations. Each makes about ¾ cup and can be used both as dressing for salads as well as marinades for fish or meat.

Whisk all ingredients together.

Try adding various ingredients to create a new twist:

Variation 1: ⅛ tsp. cumin (more to taste if you like it spicy hot)

Variation 2: Substitute black cherry juice for the water

Variation 3: 1 Tbsp. fresh mint, 1 tsp. agave

Variation 4: 1 scallion, chopped

Variation 5: 2 Tbsp. minced red onion, 2 tsp. honey, 1 tsp. grated lime peel

Variation 6: 2 Tbsp. minced garlic

Variation 7: 1 Tbsp. minced shallots, 1 Tbsp. dried parsley

Variation 8: ¼ cup crushed raspberries, 1 tsp. agave

Makes 1 cups

Ingredients

¼ cup lime juice
¼ cup olive oil
¼ cup water

VEGAN PÂTÉ

These are delicious served on their own or together, and can be paired with gluten-free crackers, crudités, or anything else you want to dip. Serve as an appetizer for your next social gathering or as a snack for the kids—no one needs to know it's so healthy!

Cannellini Bean Pâté

Mince garlic in a food processor (a mini one works well with these). Add the remaining ingredients and puree. Serve.

Sweet Pea Pâté

Puree the peas in a food processor. Add the remaining ingredients and puree. Serve.

🥄 DR. BOBBI'S PREP TIPS:

For a beautiful serving presentation, scoop the pea pâté around the perimeter of a 5-6 inch diameter serving bowl, then place the cannellini bean pâté in the center.

Feel like changing up the flavors? Go ahead. These pâtés lend themselves to many different herbs and spices, experiment with different ones on the Shopping List, including these:

For the bean pâté: cumin, tarragon and lime juice; paprika and lemon juice; curry and pears; or tamari and scallions.

For the pea pâté, replace the tarragon with basil, dill, mint, or garlic.

Makes 1 cup each

Cannellini Bean Pâté

15 oz. can cannellini beans, drained
1 Tbsp. lemon juice
1 clove garlic
1 Tbsp. olive oil

Sweet Pea Pâté

16 ounces frozen peas, thawed
1 tsp. lemon juice
1 Tbsp. olive oil
1 tsp. tarragon
¼ tsp. salt

GHEE

Ghee is the name for clarified butter in India, where it is used as a traditional healing food. The milk proteins and lactose are removed in this process, so people who cannot tolerate milk due to lactose intolerance or milk protein sensitivities generally find this is well tolerated. If you have a true milk allergy, I do not advise using ghee, as trace amounts of the milk proteins can remain.

Place butter in thick-bottomed saucepan and melt over medium heat. When it comes to a boil, you will hear it start to pop. Continue a gentle boil for about 15-20 minutes, removing any foam that forms on the top.

When the popping sound gets quieter, and the liquid becomes clear, remove from heat.

Cool for 10–15 minutes, then pour through a double layer of cheesecloth into a glass or ceramic bowl. A metal strainer, if you have one, is helpful here: Line it with the cheesecloth and set on the bowl to strain without needing an extra pair of hands.

Discard the cheesecloth and its contents. Once completely cooled, cover and store at room temperature or in the fridge.

Ghee keeps for months at room temperature.

🥄 DR. BOBBI'S PREP TIPS:

Butter is very sensitive to temperature and can burn easily. If it burns, you need to dump it out and start over. I have learned the hard way that it's best not to multi-task while making the ghee!

Makes approximately 1 cup

Ingredients

1 pound unsalted organic butter (it is important to use the unsalted kind)
Cheesecloth (for straining)

WANT MORE RECIPES?
GET CONNECTED!

Join the conversation on the following social media platforms so you can stay up to date on healthy eating using the blood type dietary guidelines and nutrigenomics, and learn about new recipes, shopping tips and other healthful tips from Dr. Bobbi and Dr. Joe of Genomic Solutions NOW!® LLC.

Be among the first to find out about new recipes and healthy tips:

Facebook: http://facebook.com/genomicsolutionsnow.com

Twitter: http://twitter.com/GenomicSolution

Learn about cutting-edge nutrition and genomics at Genomic Solutions NOW!® LLC at http://www.genomicsolutionsnow.com/

www.ingramcontent.com/pod-product-compliance
Lightning Source LLC
Chambersburg PA
CBHW061054090426
42742CB00002B/32